FINDING PURPOSE

THROUGH THE

PAIN

Lessons We Learned Through Losing Our Son

Taylor Morton

In Loving Memory of Our Son
Beckett Williams Morton

Contents

Introduction.. vii

Chapter 1   We Are Not in Control 1

Chapter 2   Love Your Spouse.. 5

Chapter 3   It's Okay to Not Be Okay 9

Chapter 4   Let People Love You.................................. 13

Chapter 5   God Provides 17

Chapter 6   God Will Be Glorified 21

Chapter 7   Keep Their Legacy Alive 25

About the Author... 29

Introduction

"We can't find a heartbeat. You're going to have to push." Words that will haunt my wife and me for the rest of our lives. On March 21st, 2021, one day before my wife Linlee was scheduled to be induced, was when those words echoed through a hospital room filled with nurses and our doctor. My wife, being the warrior she is, bared down and pushed our beautiful baby boy Beckett out with only four pushes knowing that her son would be lifeless as he left her womb.

As we held our son, we asked "why?" We were mad, we were frustrated, but most of all, we were broken. Our wonderful doctor prayed a heartfelt prayer over us. We were in the hospital for two days, and then, we went home to bury our son. My wife and I have both lost a brother, and she has lost her mother. Those were very difficult moments in our life, but this one by far was and is the most difficult one of all. Mainly, because this one didn't make sense.

My wife had the perfect pregnancy, and she had no risk factors. Yet, she suffered a partial abrasion of her placenta.

It happened on the way to the hospital. There were no underlying signs or conditions that pointed to this potentially happening. Regardless of it being a medical anomaly and it being something that rarely happens, when it happens to you it smacks you in the face and it knocks you down.

Everyday for the rest of our lives, we are going to be slowly picking up the pieces of our broken hearts and placing them back together. This book is a simple resource about what we have learned through the loss of our son. Our prayer is that it would give you hope, that it would point people to Jesus, and most importantly that it will glorify God.

CHAPTER 1

We Are Not in Control

The one thing parents want to do is protect their children. I believe that all parents should strive to protect them. That is exactly what my wife Linlee and I tried to do. Linlee studied about motherhood extensively. She took the best prenatal vitamins and had a textbook pregnancy. Her blood pressure was perfect and had zero risk factors. Absolutely none, and we still lost our baby boy.

We felt helpless and out of control. The fact of the matter was that we never were in control. God did not do this to us, but He did allow it to happen. As we held our lifeless baby, we felt like we had lost all control, but in reality, we never had it. God was in control the entire time. I am not saying we should not do everything WE can to take care of our children. We should, but there are things we cannot control.

We could control going to doctor's appointments. Linlee could control taking prenatal vitamins. We could control certain things, but we could not control the medical anomaly of a placental abrasion that was not supposed to happen. The reality is there are going to be curveballs thrown at us in life. Most of the time we are not ready for it.

We were caught off guard. I felt like the disciples that were on the boat with Jesus during the storm. The storm was raging around Linlee and me, and we felt helpless. We realized that we were not in control. We did what we only knew we could do, and that was run to our Savior and tell Him about the storm. He knows, He loves, and He cares.

The same God who controls the wind and the waves is in control of our lives. You've heard it said control what you can control and leave what you can't to God. You can control your effort - the effort you put into your marriage and the effort you put into your relationship with your Savior. Give the rest to the One who created the universe.

I am reminded of what Scripture tell us, that "His ways are not our way and His thoughts are not our thoughts." His way is best. We don't have the 30,000 foot view yet, but we are still ascending.

"The Savior commanded the wind to stop blowing and the waves to go down. The wind stopped and the sea became calm." - Luke 8:24 NLT

The same God that controls the wind and the waves is in control of your life. Even when the storm is raging all around you: He is in control.

Control what you can control and allow God to be who He is.

What can you control?

_____

_____

_____

What can you not control?

_____

_____

_____

CHAPTER 2

Love Your Spouse

L oving your spouse is something that seems normal, right? If you're not married don't tune out just yet. I hit on some ways to prepare for marriage as well. We should love our spouse, but many marriages are built around their children and not a love for one another.

Seeing my wife push a baby out that had no heartbeat and knowing that when he entered the world he would not be alive gave me a whole new respect and love for my wife. We have been through so much together, but this one - losing a child - has been the most difficult one of all.

We got married on July 22nd, 2017, and I never thought I could love my wife more than I did that day. Through the death of our son, I have found a newfound love for her. We are in this together. When I lost my brother Trent back in 2007, the hardest part for me was watching my Mom and

Dad suffer. Now, I am watching my wife go through the same thing with the death of our son.

I want to take her pain away, but I am also dealing with the sorrow as well. We are not just bound together by love but now by our sorrow. What I have learned through this whole experience is that I cannot build my marriage around anything other than Jesus and my wife. We desperately desire to be parents, but my love for my wife has grown more and more each day. I love my wife more each day.

My encouragement to you is this start now. Don't wait until you're going through a tragedy to love your spouse. Build on your marriage today. Hold your spouse tight because the day you said your wedding vows you didn't just commit to them through the good times but you also committed through the tough times. Take on the world together, commit your marriage to the King of the universe and allow Him to bless your marriage.

Men, lead. Lead your wife and your family. Point them to Jesus. Eventually the letters stop, the phone calls dwindle and the fridge is out of casseroles then you are left with your spouse. Love them and cherish them. Choose them every single day and see what God watch what God will do.

If you're not married pursue someone that will be a life partner, someone that will fight alongside you no matter what. Seek the Proverbs 31 girl. I am that lucky guy who found his. She is my do or die.

As you are seeking the Lord to provide you a spouse, be pursing relationships with family members and close friends to fight alongside you and to support you when tragedy comes. As Proverbs 17:17 encourages us: "A friend loves at all times, and a brother is born for a time of adversity" (NIV).

"But as for me and my household, we will serve the Lord." - Joshua 24:15 NIV

Make the decision right now that your house will serve the Lord in every aspect of your lives.

"For this reason a man will leave his father and mother and be united to his wife, and the two will become one flesh." - Matthew 19:5 NIV

Don't wait until you go through a tragedy to be united. Unite today, and bond over tomorrow's trials.

What is one way you can serve your spouse today?

_____

_____

_____

Who can you reach out to today? Maybe you are that person who sent the letter a few weeks ago and need to send your friend or family member a reminder that you are still here.

_____

_____

_____

CHAPTER 3

It's Okay to Not Be Okay

This pain will get easier, but it will never be okay. It is never okay to lose a child or to lose a loved one. Do not buy into the lie that it is okay. It's going to get easier. But, it is okay to not be okay.

The feelings you're feeling are normal. It's okay to hurt. It's okay to be broken hearted. If you weren't, you would not be normal. Ironically, the deeper I was pulled into the depths of pain, the deeper I was also pulled into God's love and grace, which I found to be sustaining. As the pain became more real, God also became more real to me.

My hurts were met with the tender care from the Creator, which made me trust God more. I'll never be able to explain what happened on March 21st, but somehow, I can explain that God loves me and He loves you.

No one is ever really going to understand what you are going through because every situation is different. Situations may seem similar, but they're all different. People will say dumb things, and that's okay. They love you, and that's a blessing. Don't try to make sense of it; it's the human thing to do. The reality is it doesn't make sense. This isn't supposed to happen. I would trade anything for my son to be here, and you would too.

Allow the love and the grace of God to hold you tightly. He will embrace your confusion, and He will embrace your frustration. Let the pain grow you closer to your Savior. We have a choice to make: we can stay knocked down, or we can get back up and start putting the pieces of our broken hearts back together. Allow Jesus to be the glue in which you place those pieces.

"The Lord is close to the brokenhearted and saves those who are crushed in Spirit." - Pslam 34:18 NIV

It's okay to not be okay, because our Lord and Savior is near. He is making it easier because He is near to the broken hearted. Let's be honest that is us right here and right now. His presence is near. Feel Him. Embrace Him. Trust Him.

In what ways can you rely on God more throughout this trial?

_____

_____

_____

CHAPTER 4

Let People Love You

This one is difficult for me. I am an introvert, and my wife is an extrovert. She thrives in crowds while I tend to stick to myself. But one thing that we have realized through this pain is that people want to help. People truly do care. People show how they care in different ways. Some ways may seem strange and others may frustrate you, but just know, that their hearts and their intents are pure. For instance, people will say "I'm so sorry, and I know how you feel." While they've never experienced loss in their life, or maybe they have, but no one circumstance is the same.

I would just encourage you with this thought: although their wording maybe poorly executed take a step back and know that they don't know what to say. They're just trying to comfort you in the best way that they know how. People are going to bring you so much food simply accept it and say thank you. They don't have to know you threw it out.

Give it to a neighbor or feed the homeless with it. Allow people to love you. They're simply just trying to live out the second greatest commandment by loving their neighbor as their self.

You're going to have a million texts and phone calls. Don't complain about them; be thankful someone is calling and someone is texting. You don't have to respond to every message. I would try to, but when you're ready. It took me three days to go through every text and message I had. I wanted people to know that our family felt their prayers and were very appreciative for everything. Do this on your timing. It could be the next day or it could be a few weeks from now, but let people know you're grateful for their thoughts and prayers. Communities come together in times of crisis. Take this time to be thankful for your church, for your family, and for your community. Let them love on you the way that they know how. It's hard to see past the rubble of the bomb that just went off in your life, but people showing you the love of Jesus helps clear the rubble and clear the path for brighter days to come

"He answered, 'Love the Lord your God with all your heart and with all your soul and all your strength and with all your mind'; and love your neighbor as yourself." - Luke 10:27 NIV

Let people love you; they're simply trying to show you the love of Christ. Hold tight to this thought.

Who is trying to show the love of Jesus to you? Write down some ways you can allow people to be the hands and feet of Jesus to you through this difficult time.

_____

_____

_____

CHAPTER 5

God Provides

"And my God will supply every need of yours according to his riches in glory in Christ Jesus" (Philippians 4:19 NIV). This is a verse that has been sent to me countless times since the day we lost our son. When I first received this verse, I was frustrated because I felt like He did not provide. I honestly felt like He took away, but the more and more I allowed God to move in my life, He did start to provide.

God has provided three things. These provisions have not made the death of Beckett okay, but He has made it easier. The first thing might seem unconventional, but it has been something that has taken the most difficult of pains and lightened the load. The first thing God provided is humor.

God has provided humor at the right times. From the moment we knew our son was gone to this very moment you're reading this, God has blessed us with humor. Little moments that have just put a smile on our faces. For instance, in a very somber moment when I was carrying my son in a casket to his grave, everyone was lined up. As I was passing someone who has hearing issues, I noticed that he was not looking and was just talking as loud as he could. Now, some people might think this was disrespectful, but for my wife and me, it was kind of a humorous moment. He meant no ill will; he just couldn't hear and did not realize what was going on. It was something we could laugh at later on. It made the long walk from the hearse to his burial site a little easier.

Not only has God provided humor, He has provided hope. Thankfully through His Son Jesus, we have hope that we will see Beckett again. My mother-in-law Loulee has been in Heaven since 2019, my brother-in-law Gilchrist has been there since 2015, and my brother Trent has been there since 2007. I could not help but think that Beckett was held tight by his Lolli and his uncles when he entered heaven's gates. The hope we have is that we will be reunited with him, and all that have gone before us who have a relationship with our Savior.

If you do not know Jesus, we are going to give you some information and someone to get in touch with about a saving knowledge of Jesus Christ. Our ultimate hope lies is in Jesus. We know that we will see our son again because of our Savior.

Lastly, God has provided healing. Every single night my wife and I pray, and we thank God for making the day easier than the day before. Occasionally, we will have our days that are more difficult than others, but for the most part, God is healing our broken hearts. It isn't on our time, but it's His time. God is teaching us so much through this loss, but He is providing healing every step of the way. The scars will still remain, but the scars are formed from the healing that has taken place.

Back in 2013, I was diagnosed with a cancerous tumor that was attached to my appendix and was protruding into my colon. Not only did I have an appendectomy, but I also had a right hemicolectomy. They removed my ascending colon, and the recovery (the healing process) took several weeks. But after the healing process and when I was cancer free, a pretty sick scar remains. That scar reminds me of the provision that God gave to help discover the tumor and ultimately remove it. The same applies to our pain we are experiencing in the loss of a loved one. We are healing every single day, but the scars remain. The scars will sometimes bring up difficult emotions, but other days, they will remind us of the healing provision of God. Pray for healing and always remember to look at the scars that remain to be reminded of what God has done and where He has brought you to.

"His divine power has given us everything we need for a godly life through our knowledge of him who called us by his own glory and goodness." - 2 Peter 1:3 NIV

"…God has said, "Never will I leave you; never will I forsake you." - Hebrews 13:5b NIV

God is with you! Never forget it. Even in the most difficult days, He is with you, and He cares for you. Not only is He with you; He will give you everything you need. Whether it is humor, hope, or healing, He has everything you need.

Take a moment and right down what God has provided for you? Has he provided humor, hope, or healing?

_____

_____

_____

If you need someone to speak with about your relationship with Christ call the Billy Graham Association hotline.

888-388-2683

You can also reach out to us at info@taylormorton.net, and someone will be reaching out to you and willing to pray with you.

CHAPTER 6

God Will Be Glorified

"Then Jesus said, 'Did I not tell you that if you believe, you will see the glory of God?'" (John 11:40 NIV). Our pastor, Dr. Billy Joy, has been praying this over our church for the past several months. We are slowly coming off the COVID-19 church return, and the prayer has been that we would see the glory of God. I have to believe that the life and legacy of our son's story is a part of the process of us seeing the glory of God. We are praying that God will be glorified through all of this. We have already received a text from Linlee's aunt that through the death of Beckett she was able to share the Gospel with a family member. He is already being glorified, and our prayer is that his legacy would be that we help others, point people to Jesus, and ultimately glorify God.

It's easy to the best you can be when everything is going great, but the true character of a person is found when adversity strikes. How you live on the mountain top will determine your perspective in the valley. It's easy to praise God and glorify Him on the mountain top, but will you praise Him in the valley? The valley is a great place to glorify God. Rock bottom is a great foundation to build on. Build on it for His glory. "So whether you eat or drink whatever you do, do it for the glory of God" (1 Corinthians 10:31 NIV). This "whatever you do" includes how we deal with adversity. We have a choice: will we run away from God, or will we run to him and allow Him to use our pain for His glory?

Linlee and I have around 150 students looking to us on how we will respond. Beckett was not only our baby: he was our student's baby, the staff at Valley View's baby, and our community's baby. They're broken just like we are, and they want to know what is next. Linlee and I can unequivocally say that we want to serve the Lord. We want Him to be glorified. So, every ounce in our being is going to be putting forth the effort to use the legacy of our son for the glory of God. Our perspective is that we see this pain we are going through as an opportunity, and that opportunity is to glorify our King. Beckett did not take a single breath when he entered this world, but God has given you air in your lungs for today. How will use it to glorify him?

"Consider it pure joy, my brothers and sisters, whether you face trials of many kinds, because you know the testing of your faith produces perseverance. Let perseverance finish its work so that you may be mature and complete, not lacking anything." - James 1:2-5 NIV

The pain you're experiencing right now is producing perseverance in you. It is making you into the man or woman you're called to be. Use it for His glory.

How is God using your pain for His glory?

_____

_____

_____

CHAPTER 7

Keep Their Legacy Alive

K eeping the legacy alive is something my parents taught me when my brother passed away. They started a scholarship fund in honor of him, and that scholarship has given out over $100,000 to students all over the United States. Trent's legacy has been kept alive since 2007 because of effort. It takes effort to keep their legacy alive. If you don't, no one else will. I am not saying you have to create a scholarship fund that is just what my family did. We are changing the fund's name from the "Trent McDaniel Morton Scholarship" to the "Morton Family Scholarship."

You might not create a scholarship fund, but one thing you can do is say their name. Talk about the person you have lost. Bring them up in conversations. I would encourage you to find ways to remember them, ways that can help others, point people to Jesus, and ultimately glorify God. Implement some of the things that they loved to do or were passionate about. If they loved baseball, maybe do something for kids who can't afford to play. Cover their registration fees and purchase their equipment. One thing my parents do is purchase Christmas gifts for a child in their community who is living in poverty. They spend what they'd normally spend on Trent for them. It is just another small way to keep his legacy alive, and it helps others.

We are image bearers of God, our sole purpose for existence is to know God, glorify Him, and to make Him known. We did not have the choice of losing our son, but we do have the choice of how we respond. We choose to suffer with purpose and to find purpose through the pain. As my dear friend Brent Crowe reminds us in his book *Moments til Midnight*, "We are just sojourners passing through." This is not our home; we are citizens of heaven and are on this great pilgrimage to the Heaven country. Make the pilgrimage count.

"Therefore, go and make disciples of all nations, baptizing them in the name of the Father and of the Son and of the Holy Spirit." - Matthew 28:19 NIV

Use this page to brainstorm. List as many possibilities that you can use to continue the legacy of your loved one. Keep the idea in mind that it will help others, point people to Jesus, and glorify Him .

_____

_____

_____

_____

_____

_____

_____

_____

_____

_____

_____

_____

About the Author

Taylor Morton is the author of several other books, including *It's Only Pain: But It's Real And It Hurts*, *Kingdom Leader: A 21 Day Journey To Unleash The Kingdom Leader Within Us All*, and *Penny's Purpose*. Taylor and his wife Linlee live in Moundville, Alabama with their three dogs Penny, Sophie and Willow. Linlee is an elementary school teacher in the Tuscaloosa City School system, and Taylor is a student pastor at Valley View Baptist Church in Tuscaloosa, Alabama. He is also the founder of The Morton Family Scholarship and Converge Ministries.

For more resources from Taylor Morton
visit www.taylormorton.net

CPSIA information can be obtained
at www.ICGtesting.com
Printed in the USA
BVHW080754120521
607123BV00003B/91